AF597240

MEMORIES OF LOVE ON THE BRAIN:growing your relationship passionately

TABLE OF CONTENT

CHAPTER ONE

PAY ATTENTION

It takes full-time work to love someone. Yes, I'm calling it a job as maintaining a relationship requires ongoing care. How then? Whether you like to acknowledge it or not, being in a relationship, preserving the love, organizing surprises, having sex, cleaning the dishes, interacting with family, and working as a team all take a lot of effort. You get unsatisfied because you think your spouse, girlfriend, or boyfriend isn't paying enough attention to you.

However, if you are fortunate and everything is going well, this task could appear simple. You may not even be aware of it since it will come naturally to you. And if you love someone, you will enjoy giving them your undivided attention without making it feel like work. Giving your entire attention in partnerships might, however, appear more and more difficult as a relationship progresses and the demands of responsibility pile up.

But what happens if the team or partnership isn't working well together? One or both partners may begin to feel as if they are not receiving enough attention in a relationship when the process of loving someone gets increasingly laborious. Does it imply that you must just accept an unsatisfying relationship? No, not always. You may save a relationship by consciously deciding to give it more of your time and focus. We explain how.

Why then do we place such a high value on attention in a relationship? Is paying attention to every little thing in a relationship so crucial? In a relationship, not receiving enough attention might lead your spouse to feel unwanted and uncared for.

How can you provide undivided attention in a relationship? becomes another crucial issue. Let us first define attention in a relationship before we respond to it. It entails paying attention to

and being interested in your spouse. You may use several forms of attention in a relationship to show your spouse that you are involved in their well-being and are paying attention to what they are doing.
These include romantic attention, where you show them your love and devotion, emotional attention, where you are aware of their emotional needs, and general attentiveness, where you are not distracted by your phone when your spouse approaches you to share something significant.

Due to our reliance on technology and the desire to multitask, we are unable to offer our partners our complete attention in the current world. The best scenario would be to keep your phone in your purse or pocket if you have gone out to supper. However, the boss announces a crucial call at the last second, so you continue fiddling with it in anticipation of the call.

Your spouse could find this bothersome, but they are unable to speak out since work is work.

Technoference may destroy your connection without your knowledge. In this sense, communication in a relationship is often hampered by our conduct. Most of the time, we are with our spouse physically, but psychologically, we are checking tasks off lists. Therefore, we are unable to offer a relationship as our whole focus.

How Does One Pay Attention To Someone In A Relationship?

The ritual of being a pair is ultimately only worthwhile when you both love one other. Only by paying attention to someone you love can that happen. In the absence of it, rituals designed to deepen your connection and build your bond become pointless, and the relationship begins to deteriorate. It might be the beginning of the end in certain cases, or it can be a warning that, if heard, can save a relationship.

We marry and enter into several social contracts with one another, after all, not just to have children but also for companionship and a range of other reasons. And if you're not paying attention in a relationship, what use is this company? Partners provide each other with the testimonies and opportunities we want to be heard and seen in our lives.

The fact that our companion observes, documents, and shares our lives with us makes the whole experience valuable. There are billions of us, and our lives may be lost in that turmoil. Additionally, it maintains communication within a partnership. What's the purpose of doing all of that if you feel like your spouse isn't paying enough attention to you?

So here's what you should do if you feel like you can't offer your spouse enough of your attention.

1. recognizing and heeding the silent pledge
full commitment in relationships
In a relationship, paying attention is crucial.

What transpires when our partners stop witnessing? At that point, a relationship begins to sputter and partners often start to turn away from one another. When you sense a lack of attention in a relationship, your focus shifts to other things. Your connection becomes unstable at that point. As you can see, neglecting to give your partner adequate attention may have a significant impact on your future together.

Of course, this isn't always a conscious decision, but even unconscious pulling away may be quite damaging in a relationship. The implicit commitment that couples make when they join together is to give each other their whole attention. Nobody falls in love with someone because they think them to be uninteresting.

Even if other people find their relationships uninteresting, those who are in love tend to find them engaging. I'm not advocating that our partners serve as our entertainment, but if we're going to spend the rest of our lives with them, they had better be fascinating.

2. It is more severe than we may realize.
This is precisely why being ignored by a spouse can be so upsetting that it may cause individuals to become sad and even consider suicide. Not only because their partners cease paying attention to them, but also because their lives lose purpose as a result of this lack of attention.

It might cause you to doubt your existence when the one you love the most, the one who is your sunlight and starlight, stops finding you intriguing. Because of this, you are happier with an attentive spouse and depressed with an inattentive one. It might be isolating when your spouse doesn't give you their time and attention in a relationship.

You know, some individuals give their all when they are in love; they don't hold anything back and lay everything out on the line. They believe that the potential gain justifies the risk. Ends always justify methods. They don't hold back because they believe that kind of love is untrue.

Whether you love in this manner or not, an emptiness results when someone withholds their love after offering it for a while. They may find it difficult to deal with this vacuum and it might even cause them to become clinically sad. As a result, maintaining relationships well requires careful attention to detail. It enhances communication within a partnership.

3. Social stigma makes things worse

When we consider that our culture stigmatizes mental illness and that talking about our feelings is seen as frivolous, this situation is made much worse. For a culture that enjoys rom-com melodramas, we are reserved and critical of our feelings.

People often see psychiatrists discuss how they feel neglected by their relationships but are unable to express their feelings to them. Therefore, both partners must uphold the commitment of prioritizing one another, not just during the exciting honeymoon phase of the relationship but every single day. If not getting enough attention from a boyfriend or spouse can be this harmful and attention in a relationship can hold such significant value, then both partners must keep their commitment.

4. Become unaware of the communication

People in long-term partnerships sometimes neglect communication because they are preoccupied with household duties, raising kids, and paying debts. On the sofa in the living room, they can be watching a movie together, but all they seem to care about is the popcorn. A relationship suffers from a lack of communication in such cases.

One method to show your spouse that you care is to keep each other informed of what is going on in their life. It's important to discuss your day, your children, holiday plans, and even cooking. People are connected via communication, and if you are speaking well, you won't feel forgotten. Try these communication activities if there is a communication breakdown in your relationship.

What does being alert in a relationship entail? We've now demonstrated that your relationship may suffer if you don't get enough attention. Understanding how precisely we may be attentive in a relationship and what being attentive in a relationship means is much more important. What can you do in a relationship to be more considerate?

Each interpersonal dynamic has its specific requirements for attentiveness. Being sensitive to your partner's emotions may mean different things to different couples. For some, it may simply mean preparing their favorite cuisine to demonstrate that you care.

The goal is to be sensitive to your partner's unique requirements and prevent your relationship from deteriorating. Simply said, being attentive is a method for us to convey our concern for our partners and to help them feel unique and valued. Being aware of them lets them know they have a particular place in our life.

As a result, various partners may interpret the absence of attention in a relationship differently. There are several ways in which ignorance and a lack of attention to detail in relationships may show themselves.

For one couple, failing to express their affection for one another in the morning might be just as damaging as purposeful neglect. How then can you focus more? What can you do to show your wife, spouse, or partner greater care? Let's solve the problem.

How can I focus on my spouse more?

Although each relationship is different, you can still tell when your wife or husband feels neglected in the relationship. Here are a few things you may do to fix the problem by paying attention to someone you love if that occurs:

- In every relationship, listening is critical. Our partners often feel ignored in relationships because we hear what they have to say but don't pay attention to it.
- Make plans together: Routines may sometimes give the impression that everything in your life is static, including your relationship. You can feel that your lover isn't giving you their whole attention. Make arrangements with each other to shake up the routine; these plans might be as simple as a home-cooked dinner date or a movie date.
- Do not ignore your partner's complaints, even though you may think they keep complaining about the same things. If you do this, people will see a blatant lack of interest on your part.
- Make them feel unique by recalling the times you believed you had discovered your true match. Since this is the same individual, they should be treated with respect. Plan enticing date evenings or

relive an earlier encounter. Your companion will no longer suffer from lack of attention blues after doing this.

- Plan a trip: A vacation for two that allows you to rest, relax, and strengthen your relationships is the best thing you can do to revitalize a long-term relationship.
- With most relationships, communication is the key to preserving them. It assists in dispelling any uncertainty, confirming your love for one another, and strengthening it. So, use these communication strategies to improve your communication.

What we must understand is that when there is a lack of focus in relationships, individuals may have a sensation of being left behind. Free and open discussion must become a regular occurrence. It's equally crucial that we educate ourselves on mental health issues and have more in-depth conversations about how marriage and intimate relationships have changed through time.

While we spend a lot of time teaching our children about the rivers in our country, the politics of our people, and the languages of our ancestors, we often fall short of preparing them to handle emotional issues adequately. We don't discuss the nature of love or educate children about consent. But just send them out to discover a love for themselves.

Even though every romantic experience is different and subjective, there are certain fundamental guidelines that we can all agree upon. To ensure that people continue to watch one another, we must educate them on how to communicate. If love is what keeps the world turning, then we need more clear communication to keep the world turning. especially in situations when there is a definite absence of undivided attention.

Depression, a sense of emptiness, etc. are effects of not paying attention. But inattention-related cheating is a significant issue as well. Love may be communicated verbally, nonverbally, or via concentrated attention or silently carrying out duties and taking care of family. Nowadays, when attention-seekers who are mostly selfish crooks are married, when they don't get the attention they want, they blame their spouse and start looking for people outside of the marriage, which leads to cheating (one only knows they are shameless crooks when they are exposed to tempting or difficult situations). They are equally accountable for commitment and the sanctity of marriage, but since they are self-centered scum, they don't communicate what they want or what their relationship lacks, and they don't work to fix problems. These folks exchange their bodies (male or female) with other parties seeking attention while their spouse is burning their asses for the family. What they don't realize, or even if they do, is that when there are no obligations or restrictions, any shameless, immoral person (male or female) on earth may pay attention to or make the cheater feel special while enjoying their closeness with them. Similar to this, it is best to stay away from those who are too attention-seeking and have a history of infidelity when starting a relationship. Avoiding them is preferable to having them and risking permanently burning fingertips.

CHAPTER TWO

MANAGING SUSPICION

At the beginning of a relationship, it may be difficult to recognize whether a partner is acting too suspiciously. Some behaviors, such as inquiring who you've been hanging out with or who you were on the phone with, might be misinterpreted as expressing genuine care and intense desire for your company. However, with time, such behavior degenerates into something obtrusive, intolerable, and even emotionally abusive. So, here are a few things you might try out if you think your spouse is becoming unduly suspicious.

This is not about you.

Realize right away that your partner's suspicious behavior has nothing to do with you at all. He or she may spend the whole day reading your mail or using your login to search Google, but you need to realize that this is not always an indication of how acceptable your actions are. This is just taking place because, for whatever reason, your spouse sees things differently than you do. Like chatting to a coworker after work hours may not seem like a huge deal for an emotionally mature person, but for an extremely suspicious individual, the conduct is indicative of an effort to hook up with a coworker and perhaps even a developing office romance. And because you cannot challenge someone's views or convince them that their feelings are incorrect, it is preferable to disregard such a pessimistic outlook. In truth, a person's inclination to be overly suspicious may be an extreme manifestation of their feeling of insecurity or lack of self-control, which causes them to concentrate on the alleged wrongdoings of others to feel justified in their initial suspicions. Therefore, try not to take your partner's frequent questioning personally, even if it would be difficult not to get saddened by it because it is, after all, aimed at you.

It's hard to put up with frequent misgivings from someone you love. However, avoid allowing your partner's assumptions to destroy your day or your mood. Remind yourself that no one else can affect your mood; only you do. Don't just hand this authority off like that. Additionally, remind yourself that you are in charge of your own emotions and that your partner cannot, without your permission, make you feel depressed or self-conscious.

Avoid defending oneself.

Answering yet another round of questions about who you met and what you did last night may severely test your tolerance, but try to listen quietly rather than become defensive. Prematurely cutting off your partner or responding with an irritable gesture or tone of voice will simply escalate the issue and offer your spouse more grounds for mistrust. Likewise, try not to minimize or minimize the sentiments of a jealous spouse. Not helping the situation at all is saying things like "Not that again..." or "You are insane to think like this..." These comments just make the other person feel more misunderstood. Instead, offer your spouse a chance to voice their concerns so that they feel as if they have had a chance to speak before you decide whether to take their side of the story or not.

Listen to them.

When your spouse starts to complain about your behaviors and their effects, show patience and listen to what they have to say instead of mentally shutting down or responding with counter-criticism. Telling a jealous spouse that they can communicate to you about their thoughts, that you'll listen to their worries and concerns, and that you'll attempt to understand where such bad emotions are coming from, may sometimes be helpful. Perhaps if your spouse feels understood after discussing his or her issues in a caring setting, he or she would be better able to get over such emotions and concerns.

It's natural to feel some envy, particularly while transitioning to a committed relationship (young). It has a limited range. If your spouse exhibits particularly high levels of jealousy, the relationship may be in jeopardy. If there truly isn't anything to worry about, try comforting them firmly. Consider the other person's perspective and determine honestly if their response is natural or controlling. Continue your normal course of activities after addressing the matter, assuming that you are not personally doing anything to merit a response. If the other individual won't change, you should probably find new friends.

Trust

Ask yourself, "Does he love you?" Are there trust issues your with a partner?

If the answer is yes, being patient will help you clean up the mess. Although difficult, it is worthwhile. When he realizes, it's not you. He won't ever again mistrust you in that way.

Otherwise, the response is No; kindly proceed. Not worth the effort is him.
Choose carefully.
I simply want it to cause him uncertainty or misunderstanding, which might later develop into remorse.

It would be fantastic to know what and how in a relationship makes you feel envious, but I'm going to presume you mean vague, unfounded sentiments (if there's a legitimate cause to be envious, that's another matter). The ability to trust your spouse while ignoring thoughts of jealousy or mistrust when they often surface may be quite difficult.

Talking openly and honestly with your spouse should be the first step in solving the majority of relationship issues. Inform them of your feelings and the reasons behind them. One of you may be able to alter some habits, they may provide comfort, or you may uncover underlying issues in your relationship.

After then, it might be good to keep a level head and attempt to comprehend your own emotions. What is it about particular circumstances that cause you to feel envious? Do you feel undervalued, inferior, or excluded? Try not to allow your judgment to be clouded by your feelings at the time. Breathe deeply, step back from the situation a little, and consider your feelings and the reasons behind them.

If none of that help, it may be that the relationship you're in isn't the ideal one for you. Alternatively, you might need more assistance learning to get over jealousy, in which case you should seek the advice of a therapist or relationship counselor.

I hate to be the one to tell it, but if jealousy is an issue, there is likely a significant problem that will never be fixed. Someone feels unwanted, intimidated, and inferior. The other person isn't sensitive enough, but you can't make someone else's jealousy go away. Don't go out with someone of the opposing sex unless it's a basic liking without disclosing that information. Don't invite conflict. But once someone begins spying on you, accusing you unfairly, and following you, it's all over.

CHAPTER THREE

BE HOPEFUL

Why Does Hope Matter So Much?

Hope is the desire for a result that improves your life in some manner. It not only helps to make a difficult situation in the present more tolerable, but it also has the potential to enhance our lives in the long run since hoping for a better future inspires action.

Whether we realize it or not, everyone's existence includes hope, because Everyone has dreams and aspirations.

How to Discover Your Life's Higher Purpose

What Exactly Is Hope?

Depending on who is speaking, the concept of hope might vary. When individuals use the word "hope" in a spiritual context, they may signify having confidence in a higher force and hoping for the best. They could use prayer to focus their hopes on others.

Others may see this as constantly seeing the positive side of things and viewing obstacles as opportunities.
Whatever the specifics, hope in general refers to a strong yearning for a better condition and the expectation that it will eventually come about.

Affirmations that Work for Caregivers

Optimism Is Not Hope
Optimism and hope are not the same things. In general, an optimist has more hope than others. Hope tends to be quite narrowly focused on a single problem.

For instance, "I hope I get the job I applied for," "I hope she calls," or, for a young child around the holidays, "I hope I get that bike I wanted!

How Hope Is So Important

The majority of people link hope to a grave circumstance. People want to escape challenging situations. People often find themselves sincerely wishing at that point. But hope may also be the solution to improving daily living.

That's because, according to Psychology Today, merely imagining a positive scenario—like the toddler picturing herself riding her new bike, for instance—can make someone happy in the present. It may significantly ease the burden of the current challenges.

Greater Intent

Hope is a kind of bridge that connects your history, present, and future. You envision what you want to take place. Even just imagining it may make you feel better, whether or not it happens. Hope may spur you on to take the necessary action if it's something you can partially influence, like the children fighting to escape poverty.

The basic act of being a human being depends on hope. Hope is a match in a dark tunnel, a moment of light, just enough to indicate the route ahead and eventually the way out,

Life may be challenging and hard at times. However, despite facing the difficulties of life, we humans are still ambitious and committed to achieving our most audacious ambitions.

I'll discuss the effects of adopting hope as a new strategy for reaching your objectives in this post.

1. Hope's Influence Extends Beyond Medicine
The "Placebo Effect" is a good place to start if you've ever been curious about the brain's ability. You may imagine yourself well because, according to Harvard Health, "research has demonstrated that, under the appropriate conditions, a placebo can be just as effective as standard therapies."

The mind is a strong organ that accounts for around 2% of your body weight and comprises

86 billion neurons, or "grey matter," and countless numbers of nerve fibers, or "white matter," or "axons and dendrites."

We can control hope inside the depths of the brain, which harnesses enormous amounts of processing power. According to Song Wang's research, hope is:

We understand the value of hope in our own lives, yet we lack hope regarding our objectives. This may have a significant impact on how we feel. Hopelessness is a terrible condition that leads to sadness, despair, and eventually the loss of the desire to live.

Gian Vittorio Caprara, an Italian psychologist, who discovered that optimism and hope had a significant influence on well-being when people were diagnosed with life-threatening illnesses, lends more support to this idea.

"Positivity may serve as a fundamental character trait that supports patients' attempts to effectively manage severe disease"

The risk that your life will continue to be a cycle of unmet ambitions exists even when your aspirations are not as severe as a life-threatening sickness. This may indicate that years from now you may look back on your life with regret and consider it to have been a life not well lived. That is a condition in certain ways.

Your life objectives are often well-defined, but if you are honest with yourself, you have little hope. Because, for that little instant, you envisage your life as if you had, you make lofty objectives that you know you have no chance of achieving. This hope is unfounded.

Set attainable objectives in their place and embrace the strong force of hope. You'll be astounded at the impact it makes if you set goals that you believe you can accomplish.

2. Hope for the Potential Realization

The first two qualities you would probably choose if I asked you to predict a student's academic success are intellect and ability. These would be accurate estimates.

It was long thought that aptitude and intellect would predict academic success. That, however, could not explain how certain people, whom Hanson referred to as "lost-talent," were capable of achieving high academic standards but never did so. Every young child in the world would be performing to their full capacity if academic success was based on those two tenets, but we know that is not the case.

Further research revealed that goal theory, optimism, and self-efficacy all contribute to understanding academic accomplishment. However, it wasn't the whole story; as a result, the model of hope, another motivating paradigm, was born.

Charles Richard "Rick" Snyder, a psychologist, is most recognized for his research on forgiveness and hope. He not only examined the significance of both in his research but also came up with a theory on hope in terms of someone reaching their objectives. According to his study, hope is a dynamic cognitive motivating system rather than a feeling.
Your chances of success are up if you have hope. High levels of hope boost both your chances of succeeding in your objectives and the caliber of the results you get from them.

3. The Vital Difference Between

   Optimism and hope have been correctly correlated.Although optimism implies having a good outlook on the future, it does not mandate the need for individual control over the result. In other words, positive thinking is a mental state and is not always associated with self-control. According to studies, being positive has many advantages.

increased longevity

decreased depression rates
fewer distress levels
greater ability to fight off the common cold
improved physical and psychological health
lower chance of dying from cardiovascular disease and improved cardiovascular health
improved coping mechanisms for difficulties and stressful situations
However, there is a crucial distinction between hope and optimism. A person with hope not only has the desire to accomplish their objectives, but also the plans and means to do it.

Your goal's route is crucial. The simple part is setting objectives. How often have you sat down with paper and a pen to list all the things you want to accomplish in the following two to three years? It's a never-ending addiction that, although it may feel nice at the moment, seldom leads to any real accomplishments.

You may attain your objectives with the help of hope. Hope inspires innovative thinking and the will to pursue your objectives no matter what.

The odd thing about hope is that it transcends optimism.

Patients who are near death have a great impact from hope. So it should come as no surprise that it may also improve your chances of achieving your objectives.

In this way, optimism improves the quality of academic production since it is a significant predictor of academic achievement. Each goal you select will be made up of tasks that, if you want to attain, you must do well.

Lean into the paths that will help you reach your objectives by using hope rather than optimism. Think positively and creatively.

CHAPTER FOUR

ERRATIC CONCLUSIONS

Ever tried to force your standards on someone else because you couldn't take their behavior? That is one approach to letting go of judgment, but doing so in a relationship seems like moving backward and will make your spouse feel that being who they are isn't enough.

Because of the tension and worry, we feel throughout the day, we make judgments. Negative emotions like judgments are waiting to be sparked by some form of behavior. Any close friendship is eventually tarnished by judgment because it breeds animosity.

Said with a secret wicked delight, "you're incorrect." It's incorrect to state so, however. Have you used the phrase "I feel differently"? You will likely start correcting yourself negatively when you feel the need to reprimand others.

This article will discuss the impact of the judgment on our relationships as well as what occurs when someone is expected to change from who they are to what you believe they should be.

Judgment of others begins with you

Your ability to love yourself could be greatly impacted by how you judge others around you. You will get a level of knowledge through loving and respecting yourself that will enable you to stop judging others around you.

Because they are typically the individuals we care about the most and respect their views above all else, think about how upsetting it may be to be criticized by someone we love. Consequently, hearing anything offensive come from them might seem like a knife in the back.

It is true that the way society is structured, with its constant social critique and concepts of good and wrong, may affect you. Every community and family has expectations for how we should act, what we should become as adults and other things. This tornado of expectations might cause one to forget themselves, which can subsequently result in triggered judgment.

Your hidden, buried previous emotions may catalyze judgment.

Deeply rooted emotional triggers exist in judgments. When we encounter something that we may have already experienced a long time ago, they are intensely moving sparks that ignite inside us. Extreme criticism of others may be strongly linked to many traumatic events in our history.

Anything that prompts you to pass judgment today likely has little to do with what is going on; rather, it is connected to an earlier event that sparked this response in the first place. It can remind you of how someone formerly treated you—how they bullied or ignored you—or it might be a belief you picked up in the heat of the moment because you didn't know any different.

When we are in "judgment mode," we may see the world from the perspective of a younger version of ourselves and pass judgment on things that may have harmed us in the past. Due to their dread of being evaluated again, participants in romantic relationships may distance themselves from one another as a result of harsh criticism. These "protective barriers" act as a barrier to love as well as judgment, which is where a relationship may begin to fall apart.

Love is recognizing, appreciating, and attempting to change it.
You could respond, "But I don't judge my spouse out of malice, but rather because I want to see them grow and be better.

It might be hard to transfer our ideals to other people. If the outcome is positive, then we are doing the right thing and the remarks are being made out of love rather than fear, as they would be in the event of a straightforward verdict.

It is common to support and desire to see the people closest to you succeed. This may sometimes contain some constructive criticism, but it must come from a place of love and respect rather than being sparked suddenly by anything they did or said. It should also be delivered in a normal voice.

The goal of a relationship is to accept the other person for who they are and where they are in their own life. Everyone has problems, defects, and loose ends.

But even if you believe your spouse might be more responsible and attentive, don't criticize them for their faults; instead, voice your concerns in polite conversations without smirks or other signs of sarcasm or irony.

Nobody will benefit from having a harshly critical, judgemental attitude in social interactions. You won't be happy at all if you exclusively focus on critiquing other people in your life. But how do you even know you're doing that?

A Quick Exercise to Help You Recognize and StopJudging

Consider an event that occurred to you recently and caused a significant response; it profoundly disturbed and astonished you at the same time. Even the smallest item may have a significant impact on you if you felt strongly about it.

Therefore, describe every last detail of what occurred in your own words. Avoid putting too much of your viewpoint into it. Next, let's examine the text a bit more closely. Note:

How often have you said "should" or "shouldn't"?
Examine your use of language to refer to the characters in your tale. Did you identify them in any way?
Is your voice condescending or patronizing?
You're attempting to infer what drives individuals to do particular actions.
Your criticisms
You make an effort to detail how you handled things differently.

How can a judgment be eliminated?

Long-term, the way we evaluate our loved ones' appearance, gait, spending habits, social circles, and other behaviors eats away at us. It has an impact on our sentiments and emotions. We need to stop taking our loved ones' difficulties personally, although we may not realize it.

Judging your loved one also involves being concerned about their particular behavior.

Therefore, you must first let go of control and acknowledge that you cannot influence everything they do or say. Second, you should think about having a real discussion about your problems.

Let go of the compulsion to "be correct," and have a real discussion about it. You're going to say, "Talk, talk, talk, how does that fix anything?" at this point. ”. It does, but it is difficult. You should seek advice, assistance, and a new viewpoint from THERAPY if you are unable to do the task alone because you are too preoccupied with your problems.

Through conversation, you may make sense of everything that's happening and learn to accept the defects and eccentricities of the other person. Everyone has the right to be themselves, and if anything about your partner profoundly offends you, you may let them know in a loving, secure, and connected setting. Then, you can both cross the bridge into each other's world together.

The most essential thing is to persevere, resist the temptation to pass judgment, learn to converse and have the most sincere conversation you've ever had. Through our couples therapy sessions, at 2halvesofasoul, we are here to support you with a variety of tactics and approaches that will make it easier for you. Why not make contact?

CHAPTER FIVE

INSINCERITY

In life, we engage in a lot of "games." And we play them both by ourselves and with other people. We achieve our goals via these games. They cost a pretty penny, however.

Insincerity Comes at a Cost

Healthy, close relationships are hampered by insincerity. Additionally, it hinders the pursuit of personal happiness. When you are dishonest, you deceive not just other people but also yourself. Even while we are quite skilled at such self-deception as humans, it always comes at a soul-crushing cost. Sincere people don't know who they are or the reality of their relationships with others, thus they live a life of deceit and "quiet desperation." Any connection, whether it is with another person or with oneself, suffers from insincerity. Even if the falsehood may never be "out," it will always cause harm. It holds us captive. Furthermore, as has been said several times before, it is the unadulterated truth that liberates us.

Others are more likely to trust us when we act honestly and with good intentions. But it also promotes self-confidence. And the foundation of every successful partnership is trust.

Simple Doesn't Always Mean Easy

I've been talking about the "10th Commandment," which is straightforward but by no means simple to follow. Sometimes it's just so much simpler to be untrue. It often assists us in obtaining desirable outcomes or avoiding unpleasant ones. But lying and insincerity usually come at a cost. Be as modest and true in your heart and intent as you can. Be truthful with yourself about your actions and motivations. Let your motivations be pure and clear. Have no secret objectives. Integrity requires sincerity as a requirement. And it leads to pleasure and inner tranquility.

In a partnership, affection needs to be freely given. And affectionate expression should follow suit. Being genuine is being who you are and having a child's heart. Sincerity is just plain faith. Without authenticity in a relationship, it is impossible to expect genuine displays of love. The connection becomes one-sided if love or a display of affection is denied. The balance of love has changed, and a balance of power has taken its place. And that reasoning is predicated on the idea that he who loves a partner less controls the union. The problem is that while having control over the relationship, you will experience emotional malnourishment and a lack of essential tenderness and love. In any case, someone in that relationship will begin to feel betrayed. The relationship quickly shifts from being controlled by both sides to being controlled by one person.

Sadly, you do need your partner's love. A partnership cannot be satisfied by selfish love. A relationship becomes cruel and unnecessarily painful once it reaches a selfish phase. The other person won't comprehend the connection. It will hurt him more the more he loves him. Being selfish in a relationship is fundamentally contradictory. The connection gets murky. Selflessness is the foundation of relationships in and of themselves. or the other party is not necessary. In a relationship, everything you try to get via selfishness always ends up becoming what you lose. There are fewer problems in a relationship when there is no dishonesty. There won't be any deceit.

Sincerity in a relationship results in that. You cannot attempt to plant seeds of insincerity to reap the benefits of sincerity. However, being dishonest makes one oblivious to apparent facts. Sincerity may make you blind. A dishonest person is unable to perceive herself or the consequences of her actions, even how she is endangering herself. Thus, you are unable to perceive yourself. You're just considering how to influence the connection in your favor. Furthermore, because there is no sincerity, you are unable, to be honest with yourself about your emotions for the other person. You are unable to acknowledge your emotions for the other person to yourself, which causes a chain of events. To protect yourself, you'll start transferring those sentiments onto your spouse and enforcing bizarre rules. However, you would assert that the rules are in place to control HIM in the relationship. And this sounds awful, particularly when the relationship is still new and just getting started. Before the relationship has even begun, you will ruin it. Even though you'll be aware of the reality, you won't be able to comprehend the man's avoidance of you. You will begin acting as if you are doing the other person a favor because you are unable to confess your need for them. (Remember that your lack of sincerity compels you to claim that he needs the connection more than you do.)

Unfortunately, people are put off by deceptive insincerity. Anyone who chooses to remain in a controlling relationship must be prepared to experience emotional pain. The world grows careless. The man will continue to give until he grows emotionally weary of always giving. You'll soon be on your own. You have rejected what you most need. And you are unable to accept it from yourself. You'll interpret the guy's move as him attempting to make a statement, but he's only pulling out to protect himself. He just feels pained within for you and is perplexed as to why you act in such a needless manner.

Being dishonest in a relationship is unavoidably harmful. The fact is that pride—the inability and reluctance to accept need—often underlies insincerity non a relationship. With pride, relationships don't work well. Humility is necessary for mutual surrender. Unless the relationship is short-lived, there is no downside to being open and true about your emotions. The other side is more amenable to you the more honest you are. And if he isn't sincere in return, he isn't worth your time. The pitiful thing about being insincere is that the other person can see right through your pretense of sincerity. Even though you DENY like or loving someone, it doesn't alter the fact that you do. The opposing party is transparent. You come off as being fake because of this.

Sincerity is a manufactured denial of a fact. It is the rejection of blatant truth. Yes, you might claim that by not showing him love, he will keep pursuing you. But you had best be prepared for the repercussions. Because the man will eventually quit and just your shadow will be left pursuing you. One would have assumed that the first pretense was just intended to contain him, and after you had done so, you would switch up your strategy. However, you've permanently infused the connection with a lack of love, therefore obliterating "something." At some time, you'll have to choose between being loved and gaining control in the relationship. Which do you value more? And that's all I have to say about this persistent problem.

Sincerity is essential in a marriage.

If one of the partners in the relationship is found to be dishonest, the marriage will fail. Even when they are married, one will find individuals who engage in illegal relationships in today's culture, but they never want to be in the spotlight. Here is when cheating on your life partner begins. If morality exists anyplace in society, then engaging in any secretive behavior, including a private mobile phone conversation or revealing personal information, puts one in the category of cheating and adultery.

CHAPTER SIX

DESIRE

The Porcupine Effect often causes the end of romantic relationships. Despite having a yearning for love, a person may unintentionally drive the other person away because of their concerns and uncertainties. Attempts to build an idealized notion of love often cause this. When someone wants to build or nurture a relationship, they damage it by attempting to limit it to this idealized version of love.

An event to be remembered

This film, which is regarded as one of the most romantic films ever made, illustrates what could occur when romantic ideals go wrong. Even though these expectations for relationships are formed because of fiction, real life often does not follow the joyful endings shown in romantic comedies.

In this film, Terry encounters Nickie, a notorious playboy, aboard a ship. When they first met, they were both engaged—she dutifully and he not. She was clever, and he was endearing. She first refused his advances. We still have a few days left on our journey, and I can't bear boredom, he said after persuading her many times in vain "getting her permission to join him for supper and companionship on the journey.
They were accidentally seated back-to-back at one point during the trip when they were trying to be discreet and requested single dining; when the other passengers noticed and laughed because their attempt at discretion was obvious, Terry looked down, checked herself, and pulled her stole up over her shoulder in embarrassment.
After falling in love during their brief time together, they decided to meet again in six months at the top of the Empire State Building if they could make their lives work out so that they could be together. At first, they were worried

that others on the ship would notice their attraction to one another, but they gave up when they learned that the ship's photographer was selling pictures of them together.
While Nickie was an artist, he lacked confidence in his skills and gave up painting because he never thought it was good enough. When he gave his grandmother a painting of his grandfather, he asked for her approval, indicating he hadn't done so sooner because he wasn't sure if it was acceptable. He felt he needed to establish his worthiness by being able to support himself with his paintings before asking Terry to marry him.

Nickie continued painting to show he is worthy of marriage upon her return, but he didn't want anyone to know they were his paintings because he wanted to sell them based on the quality of the painting, and not as a playboy. Unable to sell paintings, he took a job painting billboards. Eventually, he sold his first painting and started to find success. Terry broke up with her fiance and resumed singing.

Terri was hit by a car as she rushed across the street to the Empire State Building on the night they were supposed to meet; embarrassed about being paralyzed, but kept it from Nickie.
She was seated when he arrived, covering her impairment, having seen her at the ballet, he found out where she lived and came to see her on Christmas.
He said, "I painted you like that," and explained how the painting had been given to a woman in a wheelchair who couldn't afford to buy it, he took her in his arms. Breathlessly, she claimed, he said, "I painted you like that." "I can walk if you can paint. Don't you believe that anything may happen? ”

Fear of Being Rejected

The romantic themes of love at first sight, love conquering all and living happily ever after are all shown in the film. While it is typical for people with spinal cord injuries to end relationships, love triumphs in this film. Naturally, the concept of love, at first sight, is shown by a couple who fell in love within the first few days of a brief ocean cruise. The commitment to meet again in six months after making the necessary adjustments in their life illustrates the "love conquers all" motif. The idea that she will be able to walk once again now that they are together invoking the happily ever after concept at the film's conclusion.

Both Terry and Nickie had expectations based on their anxieties of rejection going into this film.

Despite being charming, attractive, and well-liked by everyone, Nickie had creative insecurities to the point that he shied away from even displaying his work to close relatives like his grandmother for fear that it wasn't good enough. He also thought Terry would reject him if he couldn't provide for them financially in the manner she was used to. He also desired for his work to be successful and accepted without the association of his well-known name, demonstrating the need for outside approval of his value (which was probably how he was used to being treated by others). Terry demonstrated rejection sensitivity by anticipating his rejection if she wasn't "complete" and mobile. This idealization of the connection reveals her conviction that a relationship is not worthwhile to pursue if it cannot be flawless.

The rejection they both dreaded was a myth. Terry envisioned Nickie rejecting her due to her handicap, and Nickie envisioned Terry rejecting him if he wasn't a wealthy artist who could support them. Both of them formed assumptions about one another without any supporting data. These presumptions almost stopped their relationship from happening and, in reality, definitely would have.

The longing for romantic love is common, right?

The need for romantic love is undoubtedly natural, just like other wants. In actuality, romantic ideals serve a function. A relationship is more likely to succeed in the beginning when there is an initial rush of emotion and romantic beliefs are held. Additionally, it is biologically necessary for people to form connections to procreate as well as to support and help one another as partners and as communities. Without romantic ideas, it could sometimes be difficult to seek partnerships. How likely are you to continue with that relationship if you had the premonition that "We're going to have problems to overcome, we will disagree and dispute, sometimes will not be able to face each other, and this for a lifetime?

So it stands to reason that the longing for romantic love is common. It is naturally ingrained in us and maintained through the myths of our cultures. The issue arises when the desire for romantic love turns into a demand rather than when the desire itself exists.

When a want turns into a demand, an unhealthy expectation is created in your life, which may have terrible effects on your relationships. Let's examine this idea of the "desire" for romantic love and how it could affect you. When you first meet someone, you may both be in the romantic stage of the relationship. In such a situation, your expectations for love may be aligned. Even so, it's feasible (probably) that your exact expectations won't match those of your spouse since passionate love has extremely definite expectations, making even that rare. Demands are likely to result in disappointment, pain, and rage as I previously said since two individuals are often not that in touch with one another. Since of the romantic idealization, your spouse could strive to live up to your precise expectations, but with time it will become harder because it is not their normal behavior.

But suppose you and your partner are in sync. Then, what happens? After the first year, if you continue to cling to your romantic aspirations, your spouse has probably advanced to the stage of mature love. If you don't accept the changes in the relationship and let go of the romantic ideals, you won't be able to appreciate or feel adult love. "He used to be so romantic! Now he wants to spend time with friends" or "She used to like listening to me speak about my hobby—now she gets bored."

Relationships are subject to unrealistic expectations due to the need for romantic love. The person envisions the "ideal" kind of love and compares all of their relationships to it. Every relationship will eventually fall short since none can last as long as the ideal romance.

In actuality, passionate love often only lasts six months to a year. Therefore, you are likely to experience disappointment and dissatisfaction in relationships until you can let go of the romantic idea and create a more enduring adult love. Relationships are unlikely to match your expectations again and time again.

People with romantic values are also more inclined to romanticize their friendships. For instance, many a bride has been disappointed when her expectations of her friends' conduct aren't met because she believes they should be as thrilled about her approaching wedding as she is. The following explains how, as a relationship develops, the desire for romantic love may become a feeling of rejection. Relationships often endure less than a year in their first passionate love period. Someone feels the loss of the "perfect" connection and feels rejected when they continue to idealize the relationship and expect it to last according to their romantic ideas. However, the emotions of rejection brought on by expecting love to adhere to these widespread idealized ideals may be replaced by the growth of mature love.

The Ideas of Romantic love

Read about this couple's experiences.
I once jokingly questioned my spouse in the early years of our relationship, "Will you love me forever?

"I'm not sure,"

“What?!!

"I erupted. How is it even possible? ”

My spouse, who is always sensible, said, "I want to love you forever. I want to adore you always. However, infinity is a long time, and I'm not sure what it will hold.

Even after that explanation, I still didn't get it. Later, when I understood what my spouse was saying, it had more value for me than the meaningless romantic reaction I had been looking for. (However, I did educate him that this is not the proper way to react to a woman's query about love.) I understood that his goal was more significant than any proclamation of love "forever."

Because he did not share my romantic perspective on relationships at the time, my attempt to elicit a passionate reaction from my spouse backfired. Only a proclamation of love forever would satisfy the romantic idea of love that I was searching for. I was disappointed, wounded, and enraged when I didn't get the "proper" reaction. My reaction was seen as a rejection by my spouse. Fortunately, I later understood the importance of "mature" love.

Numerous prevalent romantic precepts have been noted. Many of these romantic motifs may be found in fairy tales and swoon-worthy films. Shakespeare's famous love story, which has been portrayed numerous times on screen, shows Romeo falling in love with Juliette at first sight and asking, "Did my heart love till now? " Popular romantic notions include the one and only, the idealization of the partner, and the idea that love can overcome all obstacles. How many of these ideas are present in "Love"?

The only one

The idea of the only is the sentimental conviction that only one person is meant to be your true love. In this situation, you need to fall in love and know that individual at once. If one of you has had a prior relationship, you don't see them as "real" lovers but rather as temporary companions as you searched for your soul mate. The romantic notion is that once you do find your one and only, you will always come first in their life. According to the concept of a soul mate, your spouse has never loved anyone else and never will.

1) Love at "first sight." Although my spouse fell in love with me practically right away, I needed a little more time to process my thoughts. I remarked, "That's lovely, but I don't know how I feel yet," when he said, "I love you," but I think one of the reasons I did fall in love with him was because he didn't force me to feel the same as him. I recall saying to a friend, "I don't even sure whether I like him," even after we had been dating for a long. I now realize that this is because he has such a strong personality. "I adore you but I'm still not sure I like you," I now teasingly tell him.

The experience my husband had was nonetheless exceptional since love does not often blossom at first sight. It takes place after becoming buddies. After some time spent working together, it happens. It happens after repeated unplanned encounters. However, the concept of seeing someone across the room and instantly knowing they are "the one" is quite uncommon. But the Cinderella myth is a component of our romantic ideas.

2) I have never felt anything for anybody else. The boyfriend of a young lady still kept his ex-possession girlfriend in his garage. The current girlfriend thought he was disrespecting their relationship by not just giving the possessions away, even though they weren't in the way and he was waiting until his ex could arrange to get her possessions. She didn't want to be reminded that he never had affection for anybody else, not the possessions, which was the issue.

Like a spouse who disliked everything that made him think of his wife's previous marriage. Sadly, her children were involved in this. He thought that since she had previously had those "firsts" with someone else, they wouldn't be able to share them. He perceives her attention to her kids and dealing with her ex-husband for the benefit of her kids as rejection. He interferes with her connection with her ex-husband as a consequence, and he neglects her children.

This idea is a component of the "one and only" romantic idea. Any traces of previous connections that remain are wanted to be removed. They don't want to believe their lover has ever felt anything for anybody else. Alternatively, if emotions did exist, they couldn't be identical to the existing connection.

If others react by removing the former connection from their life, a mindset like this might cause emotions of rejection. For instance, a former spouse who assisted in raising his stepdaughter and wished to interact with the grandkids was warmly welcomed by the stepdaughter. But when the grandkids called him and his new wife "grandma" and "grandpa," the ex-wife (daughter's mother) felt insulted since she thought it stole her "rightful" role as the one and only grandmother from her daughter's side of the family.

All three of these individuals had a false sense of rejection, which greatly distressed them unnecessarily. None of these situations included a real rejection. But when reality didn't meet their idealized vision of being the one and only person in their loved one's life, they felt rejected.

The fact that they are no longer "in love" (and, by the way, it is always said with quotes because "no longer "in love" seems to mean something different than no longer in love) tells them that the relationship is no longer viable, which is why I've heard clients say it so frequently when talking about their feelings for their spouse, They anticipate that the intensity of being in love will never change, refusing to acknowledge that it does. These same individuals often go for that sensation elsewhere and use the fact that they are no longer "in love" as an excuse to cheat on their partner.

This viewpoint may also be seen in the need that the pair constantly experience the same level of elation and passion. For instance, a female who had been dating a guy for a few months canceled a planned date. Even though he was aware of her work-related obligations, he felt that her lack of concern or integrity was shown by this behavior. He saw her cancellation as a rejection and ended things with her since he believed she should share those sentiments and shouldn't allow anything to interfere with their time together. Although she was interested in him, she also had other duties that she took seriously and had a more mature attitude to love. She possessed integrity, but it wasn't the kind he was looking for. He always anticipated coming in top.

Some individuals devote their whole life to finding that "in love" sensation. Instead of growing into a more mature love when they no longer feel it, they terminate the relationship.

They romantically believe that the proper partnership will effortlessly sustain such sensation throughout time.

(What if)? Some individuals have such strong sentiments about the idea of the "one and only" that they have second thoughts about their affection for someone. They may even love the other person, but they have trouble committing to relationships because they are always worried that if they do, "the one I'm destined to be with will come along later—I will lose my chance."

Love is stronger than anything.
The notion that "love conquers all" denotes the conviction that, if you are genuinely in love, there won't be any issues that can't be solved with ease. It is the idea that as long as you have love, your relationship will be simple and that love is the only thing that matters. The idea is that finding the perfect partner is essential to a fulfilling relationship and that once you do, maintaining a relationship should be effortless.

In addition

1) A happy ending. If you find the perfect person, falling in love will be simple. This is the idea that if a relationship requires effort on your part, it is probably not the appropriate one. The issue with this notion is that every couple will have difficulties in their personal and romantic relationships. They risk making a self-fulfilling prophecy about the end of their relationship if they don't try to solve the issues.

2) Never had any issues. Many individuals hold the opinion that conflicts in relationships, anger against one another, and mistreatment of one another are never acceptable. Since people are fallible and will make errors, such ideal expectations are unrealistic. Consequently, sentiments get damaged even in the finest of partnerships. For instance, a woman could have felt betrayed and abandoned by her husband when she overheard him calling her a derogatory term. She thought that even though it had never occurred before although they had been together

for a very long time and he had quickly repented, he had breached their marriage and discounted the value of their connection. Such behavior, in her opinion, was a rejection of their romantic connection. Instead of examining what caused his strange conduct, the emphasis was on the emotions of rejection she experienced. As a consequence, rather than finding a solution to the issue, she persisted in harboring anger, which had a long-lasting negative impact on the nature of their relationship.

3) They must be sensitive to one another. This typically involves a demand that you and your spouse be so tuned into one another that you constantly know what each other wants without having to express it. Because of this notion, a person could experience rejection if their spouse is unaware of their needs.

A lady wants to reduce her extra hours because she feels exhausted, but her husband wants her to remain working overtime. He seems to disregard her needs, in her opinion. They haven't spoken about the problem or identified their various requirements, however. Instead, they are assuming that they are aware of one another's emotions. Because of this, they disagree while making crucial decisions.

"I shouldn't have to tell him. If he cared, he would know what I want," is a prevalent idea I see among many of my female clients. The main issue with this belief is that many men don't understand women and can't read their thoughts. But when informed what their spouse wants, they often agree to accommodate them.

For example, when Sharon complains to her husband that he ignores her, he leaves his "man cave" and spends time with her. She believes that he is simply doing it because he "should," not because he wants to. She sees it as a rejection of to need to "beg" for his attention since she feels that he "should" want to spend time with her, not as his readiness to react to her need. However, this is a wonderful illustration of how men react to direct communication since they often engage in it and comprehend it. He is thus satisfying her demand because he wants to. But first, he needed to comprehend her yearning. This illustrates how everyone has various wants, and if these requirements are not acknowledged, the other person tends to interpret their partner's needs based on their own. The amount of "together" time Sharon's husband needs may not be as great, and as a result, he may not consider her to need to spend time with him. He wants to make her happy, it's only that he doesn't know what she wants.

Again, this isn't always accurate, but the rejection-sensitive person can still maintain, "But if he doesn't feel the need to spend time with me, then he doesn't care about me." While we all have distinct needs, we often believe that others have the same needs as we do. For instance, at his wife's request, I once saw a quiet guy boost their relationship's communication. When I inquired what he did when she came home unhappy from work, he said, "I leave her alone," and when I questioned why, he explained that he prefers to be alone himself so he can think about his problems. I then inquired as to what his wife does when she notices that he is sad. When I told him that her conduct was a sign of how she wanted to be treated, he was able to be more receptive to the relationship. He wanted to provide for his wife in this circumstance, but he wasn't sure what those demands were. He was able to do so after I informed him. However, if the wife had been able to express her demands instead of feeling rejected by him, the issue may have been resolved much more quickly.

In place of romantic ideals

Knowing what to anticipate from mature love enables you to spot it when it manifests. Once acknowledged, practical expectations might take the place of romantic notions. Romantic ideals are presumably more appealing since practical expectations of love are less straightforward to define. There is no gray area in romanticism; everything is either black or white. Either he or she is your only love forever, or not. Romantic ideals forbid relationships to be messy. But to achieve it, denial is necessary. You may have to disregard the fact that your spouse was previously in love, married, and had kids. You may have to neglect other commitments. You may have to disregard individual preferences. Because the only way to keep the delusion alive is via denial.

Although it might sometimes be difficult, being open to changes in a romantic relationship and exploring alternatives has numerous benefits. In particular, you are not setting expectations for the relationship in advance and then being dissatisfied when those expectations aren't met. The ability to completely feel the other person as they are, rather than how you wish they were, is a sign of mature love.

CHAPTER SEVEN

INTERRUPTION

Getting interrupted all the time? Does your spouse or partner speak over you, cut you off, interject, or butt in when you attempt to speak to them?

It aches. It's difficult to endure being spoken over and it might make you feel inferior. It's very obvious proof that your spouse is not prioritizing listening at the time.

This individual can't care about me, you may persuade yourself, making you feel worthless. You can be disappointed about the missed chances to solve issues with your spouse since they won't (or can't?) listen to what you have to say.

Interrupting may be very damaging and harmful in a relationship. But what is happening?

Your spouse can be clueless, angry, in a foul mood, or using bullying tactics.

Someone's usual way of speaking may include interruptions.

Men and women may be raised to use language differently. Women converse to feel close and intimate. Speaking over another person is rude. Men talk to one other to learn things. Men also speak in ways that maintain or even enhance their social position. You may improve your position in the world by interrupting.

Your spouse and you both start to feel heard after you stop interjecting! However, breaking this harmful habit requires time and effort. It might be challenging to slow down and refrain from interrupting the other person when we are excited and rushing to get our point through. When this occurs, we are preoccupied with what we want to communicate and are not considering our partner's perspective or experience. The abrupt interruption and breaking off convey that your spouse is unimportant. Being cut off might make you feel as if you are invisible, your opinions are unimportant, and you are not valued. Even when the interruptions are made with the best of intentions, the message is still the wrong one.

Both sides need a place where they may express themselves and get a response to feeling connected and heard. People sometimes interrupt when they know that if they heard this one thing, the discussion would alter. Or they are so eager to show you that they hear you, but it leaves you feeling unheard, disregarded, or irrelevant (which is extremely seldom true but often believed). People will sometimes interrupt when they don't feel heard. You may maintain a sense of connection even after a chat about conflict by reminding yourself how to communicate effectively.

Here are some brief suggestions for quitting interrupting:

- Remind yourself that it is not your moment to speak. This is your partner's time to do so. Have your partner's words and their conversation in mind. Now that it is their time, your role is to just listen and make an effort to put yourself in their position. Anything unclear should be questioned to be made clear. Before you reply, summarize what your spouse stated. Ask if you can sum up what you've heard so far if the remark is longer to ensure that you're on the same page. By doing so, you'll demonstrate to your conversation partner that you're paying attention to what they have to say.

- Bite your Tongue: If you disagree or want to say anything, do it while mentally counting to 10. You could interpret the phrase "biting your tongue" literally or as clenching your fists, tensing your feet, or pinching your arm. Observe caution to avoid self-harm. Breathe deeply before you

respond. Biting your tongue will help you respond more slowly and maintain your sense of reality.

- Breathe: To settle down your agitation and keep in mind that you want your spouse to be involved in the relationship, take a deep breath. Sometimes all it takes to calm down our responses is to take a breath. Try inhaling for four seconds, holding for seven, then exhaling for eight. Breathing more slowly induces a physiological response that maintains your tranquility. Your parasympathetic nervous system is activated by deep breathing, which makes you feel comfortable and secure.
- Make a Mental Note: If anything occurs to you, make a mental note so that you may subsequently express your opinion. Take notice of the fact that your voice and your opinions matter and mention them when it is your chance to speak.
- Active Listening: Use the active listening technique. Your task at such time is to demonstrate to your companion that you are paying attention. Stop planning your next reaction and make an effort to

comprehend what your spouse is saying. Eye contact, an open body posture, head nodding, and little phrases such as "uh-huh," "ok," etc. are signs of active listening. If you can, repeat back what you have heard for clarification in a manner that shows you are inquisitive (not snarky, mocking, or irritably). Quit talking, stop the active interruptions, and begin active listening.

- Respect Your Spouse: Effective communication helps your partner feel valued, and secure, and that they are a priority for you. Make it a point to emphasize to your spouse that they are valued and that what they have to say matters while you are speaking. Keep in mind the worth of your relationship. Because you are interested in them and their experience, you want to hear what they have to say. Tell them this, please.
- Take turns: Set aside 20 minutes for debates that are unbroken, and take turns expressing your opinions. Speaking and

listening roles are alternated between two people. Exchange roles on each side. If it works in your relationship, you may use a speaking stick or a timer. Be kind; do not interrupt your companion at a point simply because the allowed time has passed.

You value your spoke much. Both their opinions and your own are valuable. Make sure they understand this by using our advice. Keep in mind that it will become easier to stop interrupting others as time goes on. Effective communication makes you feel more attracted to your mate and secure in your union.

Don't interrupt your partner anymore!

Stop interrupting your companion and pay attention instead of responding so you can hear what they're saying. Arguments may not often start in conversations between couples, but over time, tiny irritating behaviors like interrupting your spouse and failing to listen to comprehend when they are speaking can cause serious communication breakdowns.

In reality, frequent interruptions during conversations between partners are one of the main causes of so many relationships breaking down. A simple discussion may suddenly grow into a massive blowup if you are listening but don't grasp what is being said.

Have you ever observed that the happy couple always left in the setting sun after every fairytale you read or saw as a child? We've all come to understand why they stopped there and we were not able to witness what followed as we've gotten older, however. They sought to shield our young brains from the idea that even happily ever after couples have tough times, and had to cope with angry outbursts and delicate situations.

We often don't intend to be disrespectful when we interrupt someone while they are speaking. We often express our disagreement with what they say right away. However, did you know that if you do this to your spouse in a relationship, they may feel disrespected and unheard?

If this behavior continues over time, it may escalate a little fight you two have and create a split that is difficult to heal. These interruptions eventually stop being innocent and turn into a technique for you to prevent your spouse from expressing their feelings (or vice versa).

Whether it's a friendly or contentious discussion, it's crucial to make your partner feel heard and give them a chance to finish their thoughts before responding. The remainder of this post will be helpful if you've gotten to the point where every discussion ends in a quarrel over who gets to speak first.

Everyone has been interrupted at some point, whether they are at work, eating dinner with their family, or cuddling on the sofa with their significant other. You could even be accountable for it.

Even if an interruption during a conversation might be inconvenient sometimes, you usually don't notice it in the big picture. But coping with a persistent interrupter is a very other matter. Your relationship may begin to suffer from frequent interruptions, particularly if you feel like you never get to complete a thought.

Why do people nag other people?

Let's be honest. Everyone wants to be understood. And if you think you're not, the relationship may start to suffer. After all, a person's repeated interruptions not only give the impression that they don't respect you or your ideas, but they also seem to be self-centered. Interruptions may also make you feel irrelevant and inconsequential as if what you are saying is not vital enough to be heard.

Some interruption tendencies are a result of racial and familial histories. To them, interfering simply comes naturally. Other interrupters, on the other hand, are impatient, goal-oriented individuals who want to get right to the point. And their method for doing that is to interject and take over the discourse.

Some individuals interrupt because they want to add their ideas and emotions to what you are saying but can't wait for you to finish.

Similar to habitual interrupters, many may not even realize they are doing it. They believe that the discussion is exciting and lively because of their habit of interrupting others.
Chronic interrupters are also using your time to express their authority, expertise, and opinions, whether they realize it or not. Interrupting may also be anything else than helpful in dire circumstances. In reality, emotionally abusive individuals often use interruption as a strategy to establish dominance and control. It's crucial to learn how to deal with interruptions politely and dignifiedly while still being able to communicate your message.

CHAPTER EIGHT

FEAR

Although falling in love may be joyful and exciting, for many individuals it can also be frightening, because of trust issues. What if it is damaged? If you're terrified of love, you could be more afraid of being weak, being wounded, being left behind, or failing. In extreme circumstances, this fear may manifest as philophobia, a condition marked by intense anxiety and severe mental or physical suffering (chest aches, trouble breathing, nausea, panic).

Regardless matter the severity of your fear, there are several strategies to overcome it and enable yourself to share pleasure with someone you care about. You must first identify what is causing you to hang on before you can learn to let go. Because of past heartbreak, some of us turn away from love, but for others, the issue is

more complicated. Do we dread partnerships because of problems with our own identities or because we think the other person won't feel the same way about us?
You may be feeling fear in your relationship and finding it difficult to restrain your negative emotions for a variety of reasons. Sometimes the cause might be hidden difficulties with unresolved anger in your relationship, or your dread can be a result of potential emotional desertion.

Depending on the source of your anxiety, there are methods to put things right, start the healing process, and rebuild lost trust—all of which will make you feel safe and comfortable in your relationship. Therefore, before attending a class on relationship-building skills, it's crucial to look more closely at the possible causes of your worries and what you can do to maybe overcome them.

Why do I feel anxious in my relationship?

There are times when being terrified in a relationship has nothing to do with bad treatment or unpleasant sentiments. It can just imply that you're afraid of falling in love, being vulnerable, and all the other things that being in a committed relationship might entail. Let's look at the most typical causes of relationship apprehension:

You're worried about seeming weak since entering into a new relationship might feel perilous. New partnerships are often unexplored waters. Your fundamental defenses are put to the test, making you fear that you may be exposed and defenseless.

You're terrified of being wounded again: Your prior romantic history and ancient family scars may be influencing your present romantic experience. Your capacity to commit may be affected by the pain you may have had in your prior intimate relationships since you may be afraid of being hurt again.

You're concerned that love will undermine your sense of self: Being in a committed, loving relationship might cause some individuals to worry that they will lose their sense of self. They fear that their relationship may alter and sway their perceptions of who they are as people.

You're terrified of the suffering that comes with love: You could be worried that the whole delight of being in a relationship will be ruined by the inevitable melancholy that comes afterward.

You worry that your love won't be returned to you in the same measure as it does to your spouse, or you worry that you won't show them the same level of commitment and affection that they show you.

You're worried about losing contact with your family: Some individuals think that forming long-term relationships is the first step toward severing your ties to your family and moving further away from them than you'd prefer.

What Is It Called, When You Fear Relationships?

No matter how lovely and inspiring it is, love can sometimes be frightful, and some dread is quite acceptable and anticipated. However, philophobia, or the dread of loving and bonding with another person, is a severe fear of relationships that may manifest itself in certain people.

The dread of allowing oneself to fall in love is known as philophobia. Symptoms may differ from person to person, and even if you don't have this ailment, you could still have symptoms that you need to address and treat. Most photophobic individuals recognize the following typical symptoms:

- You find it hard to forgive the past.
- You worry that your heart will be shattered.
- You're not letting people in.
- You often struggle with trust.
- You're too preoccupied with being single.
- When you're in a relationship, you feel like you're in a cage.

- You're simply taking pleasure in a relationship's physical elements.

How Can You Conquer Your Fears?

When attempting to be a part of a loving, supporting, and caring relationship, learning how to overcome your fear of relationships is essential. Before trying to conquer your fear, three preliminary stages must be completed. Despite how foolish they may seem, they are essential for the first efforts:

1. Make an effort to acknowledge that you are feeling relationship dread and work try.
2. Look for the fundamental cause of your relationship phobias.
3. Choose to try to get over your relationship phobias.
4. Additionally, do not hesitate to get in touch with knowledgeable and experienced relationship coaches who can assist you in identifying and overcoming

your relationship phobia. You may always seek the help of specialists if you're having trouble solving your issues on your own.

How To Overcome Your Fears

You may strive to overcome your relationship anxieties once you become aware of them. Although there are various approaches and stages to truly getting over them, you may always attempt the five steps below, which are easy yet comprehensive and powerful:

History
Look back on your dating past, the reasons why your relationships ended, the main obstacles and roadblocks, and make some inferences.

Internal judge
Do not let your own unjustified emotions of inadequacy interfere with your ability to have a satisfying relationship.

Defenses
Examine your possible defensiveness, attempt to understand why it could be there, and if the justifications don't hold up, dispute them.

Feelings
Give yourself permission to fully feel and encounter all the wonderful emotions that a committed relationship has to offer. Keep your eyes open for the beauty of a loving connection.

Vulnerability
Then, without attempting to defend yourself by shutting up, let yourself become open and welcome the inherent vulnerability that follows.

the serious phobia that destroys relationships

1. "He/she is leaving me," you say.

Do you have a gut feeling that the individuals you depend on for connection and support are unstable or unreliable? If you feel that your friends, family, or spouse aren't giving you the support you need, it's crucial to follow your instincts.

However, consider if your reaction is a result of a strong fear of abandonment or whether you feel unsupported.
People who love you will forsake you or die, are typical ideas you experience if you dread abandonment. I've never had somebody there for me. The closest friends I've had are unpredictable. I'll be left alone in the end.

You have the propensity to extrapolate and interpret the actions of others around you. Because of your victim mentality:

You could start to clutch.
To test the relationship, you may intentionally or subconsciously cause disputes. (This may become a self-fulfilling prophecy; you may drive people away so often that they do abandon you.)

You engage in relationships with unavailable individuals (e.g., they live in a different location, they are in another relationship, you have incompatible schedules, and so on).
You stay away from others so you won't be left behind.

2. I simply have a feeling I'm going to be harmed.

You are likely to be able to relate to this constant worry of being severely wounded if you were raised in an atmosphere where you felt unsafe, didn't trust your friends and family, or were the victim of abuse.

You can have circular thinking patterns such as, "I constantly get wounded by the people close to me." If I don't defend myself, others will take advantage of me. Those I trust mistreat me. Therefore, as a consequence of your pessimistic outlook:

You are continuously on the lookout for any indication of abuse or treachery.

When you are the recipient of kindness, you wonder whether there is a hidden agenda.

Being vulnerable is tough for you, if not impossible.

You try to keep others from becoming upset by being agreeable and obedient.

You strike out at others to defend yourself from the abuse you anticipate.

You stay away from others because you're afraid they'll harm you.

Because no one can be trusted, you steer clear of connections.

3. "When I need him/her, he/she won't be there for me,"

You probably expect emotional deprivation in your adult life if you don't get enough emotional support, attention, love, direction, or understanding when you're growing up. I don't receive the affection I need, which is among the thoughts that accompany this anxiety. Nobody in my life cares about me or takes care of my emotional needs. I have no strong emotional ties to anybody.

As a consequence of believing that you will always be alone:

When you don't obtain what you need, you become irate and demanding.
People who don't show their feelings attract you since they help you feel more alone.
You don't talk to others because you're afraid they won't like what you have to say (e.g., lack of validation or interest).
Because you aren't receiving the love and understanding that you need, you instantly become resentful of other people.

4. "I'm not up to par."

Your thoughts may include: If people truly knew me, they would reject me if I feel awful, worthless, flawed, or unlovable. I am not deserving of love. I'm ashamed of my shortcomings. I put up a fake front because I know that if people knew who I was, they wouldn't like me. You feel inadequate, and as a result:

- People who are critical of you attract your attention.
- You make them seem bad.
- You mask who you are.
- You want to be assured.
- You find it hard to take criticism.
- You make negative comparisons to other people.

5. "I have failed."

The last significant concern that may destroy your relationships is the conviction that failure is inevitable or that you fall short of your peers because you aren't as brilliant, successful, or intelligent as they are.

You could think, "Most of my peers are more successful than I am," in this situation. In my life, I am not as intelligent as other individuals. I'm embarrassed that I fall short of others. I don't have any particular abilities. Because of your intense self-doubt:

You steer clear of conversations or circumstances where others could be compared to you.
You enable people to belittle your achievements or criticize you.
You undervalue your abilities or potential.
For fear of being seen as a failure, you conceal your genuine nature.
You condemn and judge others.
The good news is that you don't have to let these concerns ruin your relationships any longer. Being aware is the first step in changing your connections such that you feel fed and supported by them. By first recognizing your misgivings, along with the ideas and actions that go along with them, you may empower yourself. From

there, you may start to change your behaviors and add more awareness to your life.

Stop right now and force yourself to be in the present. Recognize that your anxieties and the ideas they bring about are bringing you back to a mentality or previous experience that has given you a mistaken perspective. Delay your response since doing so will cause it to become twisted as well.

Give yourself enough time to control your urge for personal development and transformation. Take in your sensations and ideas without trying to control or evaluate them. Once that emotional storm has gone and you can see that this current scenario may not be related to the worries you are projecting onto it, you can then react in a manner that is beneficial to your current relationship rather than destructive.

CHAPTER NINE

COURAGE

Everybody wants their relationships to succeed. You'll need guts if you want to maintain the strength of your connection. Yes, you probably believe, we'll need guts to overcome hardships together. True. But to continue loving your spouse, you'll also need bravery.

Loyalty, faithfulness, overcoming obstacles together, having fun together, enjoying sex, and experiencing the satisfaction and safety of each other's presence are what most individuals see for the future of their relationship.

What often escapes your thoughts is what will be necessary for you to truly realize your aspirations. And that takes bravery.

Every marriage sometimes feels bitterness and unhappiness. Relationship frustrations sometimes stem from differences that seem to be incompatible—feeling scrutinized, lonely, smothered, scolded, or sexually dissatisfied. Too often, spouses just give up.

We are not as immediately and passionately stimulated during courting. Simply said, the stakes aren't high enough yet. Your spouse gains a lot more significance as your connection deepens.

Because they are now "under your skin," once you enter a committed relationship, your spouse has the power to make you feel threatened. They now can make you feel insignificant, constricted, or alone and abandoned. The tension that builds up gradually is caused by this innate tendency to feel threatened and to pose a danger, and it takes a lot of fortitude to dispel it.

Intense reactions are your cue to go a little further into the reasons why you and your spouse are at odds. You may not instantly recognize these sources since everything is happening in your "lizard" brain. Your survival instincts, which cause "fight or flight" reactions, are housed in this primordial portion of your brain.

When you respond adversely to anything, a burst of emotion emerges that quickly reaches into a reservoir of pain you have already experienced. This greatly fuels the fire that is already burning.

Why Bravery Is Required for a Truly Happy Relationship

Taking on your unpleasant feelings might result in happiness.
You'll need guts if you want to maintain the strength of your connection. Yes, you probably believe, we'll need guts to overcome hardships together. True. But to continue loving your spouse, you'll also need bravery.

Loyalty, faithfulness, overcoming obstacles together, having fun together, enjoying sex, and experiencing the satisfaction and safety of each other's presence are what most individuals see for the future of their relationship.

What often escapes your thoughts is what will be necessary for you to truly realize your aspirations. And that takes bravery.

You may decide to accept the fact that such emotions will never change. However, the answers you sometimes choose (such as "I'll try not to become too upset" or "I'll simply accept things as they are") may be abandoned in an instant.

You lose all of your determination in an instant. Even apparently little matters might cause you to respond in a manner that you later recognize was illogical.

If, for instance, you had regular criticism from your parents, you probably have a reservoir of unpleasant emotions stashed away, typically containing guilt or self-doubt. You may respond defensively in an instant if your spouse criticizes you, even in a little manner, to shield yourself from a wave of unpleasant memories from the past.

Your response is more about the past than it is about the present. Additionally, it causes your love relationship to seem distant and disconnected.

Show me a man who can listen to a woman without trying to solve her problem but simply listen to her and be there for her, and show me a woman who can sit with a man who shares this vulnerability and still love him for who he is. Then I will show you a man and a woman who are brave and have completed their work.

When we own our flaws and let people share those parts of our narrative, there is a huge depth of beauty.

No one, male or female, is flawless. We cultivate a narrative that says differently although we are aware of the truth. Our desire to endure the messy and, at times, taxing effort of being vulnerable and improving through our flaws is overcome by the appeal of fitting in and being accepted.

I see a few significant differences from how bravery is perceived in our society based on this. True bravery has nothing to do with the heroic or with achievement. You could have been married for 40 years, but you've never shown bravery.

Additionally, courage is neither careless nor inadvertent. Courage does not tolerate foolishness, and it cannot be discovered in individuals who make little effort and depend only on their innate or subconscious inclinations.

Courage is a determined effort. It is the particular readiness to discipline your thoughts to do something challenging, knowing that the results are unclear, and nevertheless being prepared to go on your trip in the hope of a better future.

The persistent weakness of courage. It overpowers the selfish voice within your head that nags at you to stop being so brave since it puts your safety in danger.

Your instinct to protect yourself will make an effort to persuade you that having bravery is risky. It is in error.
The biggest threat you will ever face is a life devoid of bravery, a life that is hesitant or, worse, reluctant to enter a vulnerable place and come out on the other side transformed for the better.

We need more guys who understand the worth of genuine bravery. We need more female role models who honor those displays of genuine bravery. Our culture requires it. For you and me individually, it is necessary for our relationships.

For Men: Courage

"Courage is not having the power to continue; it is continuing even when you are weak." Roosevelt, Theodore

Throughout history, mankind has distorted the concept of bravery and twisted it toward success and heroism. Boys are taught to battle dragons and save princesses as they grow up, and we create imaginary worlds where these heroic deeds are rewarded with trophies that might be real or imagined.

The realization that these same young boys carry an ideology and concept of bravery that is based on heroics and is motivated by reward as they develop and grow into men is not a weird conclusion from this.

Does that describe any males you know?

As a result, mature men are predisposed to accept the motto "If I can repair it in my power, I will win" as their definition of bravery.

But in a genuine relationship, it isn't what true bravery entails.

According to Theodore Roosevelt, having bravery is moving on even when you lack strength. even though you're weak. However, in a society where power and bravery are often equated, weakness is considered something to be eradicated rather than cherished.

As a consequence, a lot of guys are taught that being strong entails repressing feelings and having no sensitivity. Not at all.

True strength is the capacity to equate bravery with frailty. It is realizing that you are worthy and deserving of love even when all of your strength is gone.
That is a male perspective on bravery.

This implies that I must be prepared to value my wife's opinions, respect her feelings, and accept the fact that I am not the marriage's savior. I am an equal participant who needs the advice I seem to want to provide just as much.

Men must be ready to let go of the rescuer complex if they want to mature and progress in genuine relationships. We are not repairmen. Even if our younger imaginations would attempt to argue otherwise, winning kingdoms is not the source of bravery. It results from our defeating ourselves.

Female Courage

Being courageous is experiencing fear and moving on despite it, not being fearless. Try interpreting your dread as a hint that something significant is about to happen. Gloria Steinem.

Recently, there has been a greater deliberate emphasis on the bravery that women show when they challenge outdated social and cultural standards in their quest to transform the world.

More bravery like that is needed, and there is still much work to be done in this area.

But when it comes to relationships, we also need to see an increase in other kinds of bravery in addition to this one.

Show me a woman who can sit with a guy who is vulnerable and yet love him for who he is, as Brene Brown said above.

When it comes to emotional maturity and intellect, women have traditionally been at the tip of the spear. With such influence comes the need to guide men into a deeper and richer degree of vulnerability while avoiding the trappings of manipulation.

Strong, independent women build relationships based on hope, belief, and value in their partners' character rather than their achievements when they are willing to be bold and praise their partners' acts of vulnerability.

The process of listening and encouraging women might seem difficult because they have fought for so long just to be heard and appreciated in the right ways.

For years, we've been trying to dispel the perception that women are just princesses in need of saving. This is true, but it may also be misconstrued to support a mentality that equates boldness with gaining independence and power.

It takes tremendous bravery for women to understand that allowing their spouse to have dignity does not imply a loss of power in the relationship. Sitting next to someone when they are vulnerable doesn't make you less than them. Selfless love is not frailty.

My wife has been kind, accommodating, and gracious as I've tried to be better at talking about my feelings. She often reminds me that improvement is preferable to perfection. She has evolved into the safest place I have ever known due to her bravery.

The most powerful force you have to give is this love. This love fosters friendship that is based on equality and respect in relationships and grounds optimism for the future on a foundation that endures no matter what happens. Such bravery is admirable.

The world of self-denial
When it comes down to it, bravery is the desire to keep trying even when it seems risky or goes against our interests.

Ultimately, selflessness is the foundation of bravery. Our propensity for self-focus is overcome by courage, which advances into the domain of self-sacrifice.

While courage requires effort, it is always worthwhile. True bravery reveals new degrees of vulnerability, stabilizes these levels, and stokes fresh feelings of awe and thankfulness.
Will you have the guts to prioritize bravery in your relationship?

The Courage to Connect: What It Takes and How Intimacy Feels

There is a lot of misunderstanding regarding intimacy, including what it is and how to get it. Some long-married couples can be physically close yet struggle with emotional intimacy. Your innermost self is referred to as being intimate. Most often, people assume it refers to having sex or discussing private information. True closeness entails much more. It gives us a sense of fulfillment, control, wholeness, tranquility, and happiness. It nourishes and changes us. A partnership has to have physical intimacy, communication, sex, and romance, but mental intimacy also gives it new life.

Partners often experience emotional abandonment, boredom, and a loss of sex drive due to a lack of closeness, which is referred to as "inhibited sexual desire." Couples who dread intimacy may become emotionally distant from one another and engage in a never-ending cycle of closeness and distance.

Intimacy needs trust and safety for you to feel free to let go and be who you are. You must be conscious of your inner experience in the present and possess the bravery and willingness to express how you are feeling to someone who likewise experiences similar deep sensations.

Being honest and forthright is made possible by self-worth. The more confident you are in yourself and, ironically, the more independent and distinct you can be, the more open and receptive you are to intimacy. There are, in fact, several degrees of closeness.

You provide personal information at the entry-level. It can be information that you deem private or family-only information. Many individuals rapidly get attached to strangers. In the hopes that a partnership would increase their self-esteem and provide them satisfaction, they wish to integrate to feel whole. According to studies, even strangers who converse about personal matters for a half-hour might fall in love after four minutes of eye contact. However, intimacy is being near someone, not merging. The majority of individuals, particularly codependents (who make up the majority in America), conflate closeness and love with sharing and attachment.

You share emotions at the second level, which is the level that characterizes intimate relationships, but not feelings about yourself, each other, or current events. Most people would consider this to be quite personal, and at this point in their relationship—or earlier—couples often begin having intercourse.

There isn't much danger involved when you communicate your sentiments about your job, family, or an ex, for example. This is different from sharing your feelings about yourself. At this stage, sex may not elicit feelings of closeness and may even be used to avoid connection. Afterward, you can have an emptying sensation rather than a sense of safety and closeness. True intimacy demands the kind of trust that comes from getting to know someone. You don't frequently get to do this with someone you've just met. On an aircraft, you may tell a stranger everything about yourself, but you wouldn't say what you thought of them or yourself, which would need a greater degree of intimacy.

You become more forthcoming and candid with your sentiments as you reach the third stage. For most individuals, this is quite personal, although it lacks certain qualities of true closeness. You could not be expressing deeper emotions that aren't necessarily related to what's going on, or there might not be any reciprocity. Saying that you are proud, guilty, or humiliated about something is an example.

More protection is needed when the sentiments are negative since there is a higher fear of rejection. When meeting or dating someone for the first time, individuals sometimes disclose unfavorable information and sentiments about themselves. It's generally not in a private setting and is intended to make you want to break up with them or determine whether you still want to date them. Another example would be talking about your emotions with someone you won't see again while in a workshop or flying.

One codependent will listen while the other expresses sentiments over a situation. While sharing each other's suffering and issues might seem close, managing or providing care for the other person disregards their autonomy and separateness. It has been referred to as pseudo-intimacy and lacks mutuality.

The Secret to True Intimacy

Genuine closeness calls for authenticity, which is being truthful in the present. It's not about discussing your history or troubles; rather, it's about how you feel about yourself, how things are going right now, or how you feel about the person you're with. It has a strong sense of immediateness. Understanding your emotions is vital. Our judgments and ideas are not emotions. It takes presence and awareness to connect with true, honest sentiments in the present. Additionally, you need to be confident while promoting yourself.

To feel confident about yourself and be able to be yourself without worrying about being rejected or condemned, you must have self-esteem. If not genuine, stating "I love you" might be less personal than saying "I don't love you." Sugarcoating the truth prevents you from experiencing the wonderful connection that comes with it. It takes guts, particularly when you say something that can make the other person uncomfortable. People know they can trust your honesty, and your connections expand as a result. It has the opposite impact unless you intend to stop the relationship.

You're accepting that you're two different adults sharing your own experiences and respecting those differences, as opposed to merging or pretending that differences don't exist to feel accepted. Autonomy enters into this situation. You must be confident in your ability to thrive alone; otherwise, you will hold back on your disclosures out of fear of losing the relationship or yourself.

In conclusion, although private discussions vary in degree of closeness, the most intimate ones necessitate:

a sincere presentation of one's sentiments rather than knowledge.
feelings that are now occurring.
that you respect each other's individuality.
Whether the emotions are directed at you or the companion.
You may start by letting the person you're with know that you want to feel closer but are unsure of how or what to say if you want to do this but don't know how. If you acknowledge this when it occurs to you, it is an honest acknowledgment and the start of intimacy.

www.ingramcontent.com/pod-product-compliance
Lightning Source LLC
LaVergne TN
LVHW012118170826
845678LV00014BA/3000

* 9 7 9 8 3 5 9 3 9 4 4 9 9 *